I0486590

How to LIVE on Minimum Wage
Maximizing you life on a minimal income

Tiffany Green

Published by Lulu

Disclaimer

Information herein was gathered from sources believed to be reliable, but cannot be
guaranteed to remain current or to apply to any particular individual's circumstances.
The suggestions in this book are opinions of the author. This book is sold with the
understanding that the author is not engaged in rendering legal, financial, tax or other
professional advice or services.

The author, publishers and distributors specifically disclaim any liability, loss or risk –
personal or otherwise – incurred as a consequence directly or indirectly of the use
and/or application of the techniques or contents herein. You are urged to seek out the
services of a competent professional to be certain the information contained within is
appropriate to your situation.

All product and company names herein are copyright of their respective owners, none
of which have sponsored or endorsed this publication.

Printed in United States of America.
10 9 8 7 6 5 4 3 2 1

For information about special discounts for bulk purchases,
Please contact Mazulio Publications at bulk@mazuliopub.com
www.lulu.com/mazuliopub

ISBN 1-4116-3630-9

To my grandparents,
Monroe and Georgia Lee Williams
for maximizing their lives

Congratulations on making the decision to LIVE!

Since you have purchased this book, or received it from a caring friend or relative, you are obviously tired of being broke and living a minimal life.

You may or may not be earning minimum wage but you find yourself working extremely hard to stay afloat without enjoying life.

Well, no more!

You now have a guide for less than five cents per day, to help you maximize your life on your minimal income.

TABLE OF CONTENTS

SHARING MY STORY

SHARING MY STORY

You may have heard people say that as long as you have a job, you should be able to meet your basic needs.

I must confess that I was once one of those people.

That was before I quit my "good paying job" in Louisiana to attend school full-time in Georgia.

No family to lean on (none that I know well). No friends to borrow from (or any that had money to lend).

WHAT WAS I THINKING?

With little worry, I concentrated on achieving a new educational and career goal. However, very soon my savings ran low. Then it ran out. It was time to get a job.

Yes, there are plenty of jobs around but those willing to work with my class schedule did not pay enough to cover rent, food, clothing, medical insurance, car note, tuition, credit card bills and loans. Not to mention my new city was full of concerts, plays, festivals, restaurants and clubs that I could not afford.

Let's fast forward to me working two part-time jobs while taking six classes.

What was my idea of adding balance to my life?

Watching television re-runs, reading books and magazines, and paying bank overdraft fees to finance an occasional dinner or movie.

Almost a year later, I decided to begin enjoying my new city and bring some real balance into my life. You can't put in 40 hours per week just to pay bills!

So, as a Communications major I did a little research and then decided to share some of what I learned. Web sites, books and other sources inspired many of the ideas and suggestions provided in this guide. This information is in the "Resources" section.

So, sit back, relax and enjoy!!

DEFINING MINIMUM WAGE

DEFINING MINIMUM WAGE

As I said earlier, you can find yourself living paycheck to paycheck without a minimum wage salary. However, for the purposes of this book, we will use the federal minimum wage of $5.15 per hour as our gauge.

All calculations and information are based on a 40-hour workweek as shown below:

$$40 \text{ hours} \times \$5.15 = \$206 \text{ per week}$$
$$52 \text{ weeks} \times \$206 = \$10,712 \text{ per year}$$

Brace yourself…

You have approximately $892.67[*] per month to meet your financial obligations and create a balanced life.

[*] before taxes

FINDING A PLACE TO STAY

FINDING A PLACE TO STAY

Experts recommend you budget no more than 40 percent for housing. Following their advice, you have $357.07 per month for housing. So, we will start with that amount.

RENTING

Renting a place to live can be nerve-racking for anyone regardless of income but it can be rather scary for a person making minimum wage. Let me show you what I mean.

Many apartment complexes require tenants to make **three** times the monthly rent. Your salary of $892.67 per month qualifies you for $297.33.

You probably don't want to think about the neighborhood you will live in with rents less than $300 per month.

Due to your income, you probably qualify for rent assistance programs offered by the U.S. Department of Housing and Urban Development's (HUD) Housing Choice Vouchers Program.

HUD's Tenant Based Vouchers program may be of interest due to its flexibility. This program allows qualified families and individuals to choose privately owned rental housing instead of public housing projects.

The vouchers pay the difference between 30 percent of your adjusted family income and the local Public Housing Authority's determined payment standard for rent in your area.

EXAMPLE: $892.67 salary per month x 30% = $267.80
$500 rent standard - $267.80 = $232.20 voucher

Call or visit your local Public Housing Authority for requirements and other voucher program information.

If government rent assistance isn't your cup of tea, don't worry there are other options. As with all choices in life, there are pros and cons. Here are just a few:

Option 1: Live with a relative
Pros:
- No rent or low rent
- Less spent on food and toiletries
- May provide transportation

Cons:
- Requires you to run errands
- Gossip with other relatives about your actions
- If it doesn't work out may damage relationship

Option 2: Find a roommate
Pros:
- Lower rent and utilities
- Better apartment/house
  - 1 roommate up to $714/month
  - 2 roommates up to $1071/month
  - 3 roommates up to $1428/month
- Possibly, avoid strict income requirements

Cons:
- Late on their ½ of rent
- Unwanted guests
- Clash of personalities

Option 3: Rent a room
Pros:
- Low rent
- No long-term contracts
- Avoid strict income requirements

Cons:
- No contract can be asked to leave at anytime
- Hard to check references
- Somewhat difficult to locate

Whatever option you choose, be sure to discuss the terms of your living arrangement. Experts recommend putting together a written roommate agreement. It also would be a great idea to do the same if you choose to live with a relative.

A few things you may want to include in your rental agreement:

- Rental amount and date due
- Penalty amount for late payment
- Rules regarding time in/out of home, guests (especially overnight guests), household cleaning/chores
- Any other items that could potentially be a problem

OWNING

Don't look so surprised! You really can own a home. Of course, at your current wage a lender would probably want you to show at least two years of consistent employment. Nevertheless, the most important thing is the possibility.

In addition to rental assistance, HUD provides information on down payment assistance programs. These programs can provide enough money to increase the amount of home you can afford.

Plugging your salary into the mortgage pre-qualification tool at www.ginniemae.gov you find:

	FHA Regular Loan	Conventional Loan
Max Sales price*	$34,236	$42,268
Closing cost	$340	$2190
Down Payment	$1027	$6340
Monthly Payment	$259 (5.625%, 30 years)	$294 (5.75%, 30 years)

* Assumptions: 1) no outstanding loans, child support or alimony payments 2) credit issues are resolved

As you can see, homes backed by HUD (FHA loans) require much lower out of pocket costs than conventional loans. They also allow more flexibility when qualifying.

You may say you cannot find a home at this price in your area but, houses and condominiums listed through HUD often sell below their appraisal prices or a lower prices than you will find on the market.

Although sold in an "as-is" condition, certain HUD homes provide money allowances at closing for small repairs. There are also home rehabilitation programs through HUD, which many extremely low priced homes require.

You can explore purchasing a home with a family member or close friend to qualify for a larger home or duplex. Be sure to draw up a written agreement or contracts before entering such arrangements. Plugging the combined salary of two minimum wage earners into the mortgage pre-qualification tool at www.ginniemae.gov you find:

	FHA Regular Loan	Conventional Loan
Max Sales price*	$67,473	$83,304
Closing cost	$669	$3403
Down Payment	$2024	$12,496
Monthly Payment	$510 (5.625%, 30 years)	$580 (5.75%, 30 years)

* Assumptions: 1) no outstanding loans, child support or alimony payments 2) credit issues are resolved

Additionally, other state and national programs provide housing counseling and down payment assistance to low-income earners. You may be able to combine assistance provided by these programs to afford a larger home.

As with any housing programs, please contact your local Better Business Bureau and HUD office for the company's record. You should also ask for proof that they have helped other low-income earners in your city. Ask additional questions such as, what type of homes and in what neighborhoods their participants have purchased. In other words, do your homework!

Find out everything the programs require of you up front and if you are required to contribute any money. If so, inquire whether there are recommended down payment assistance programs available that require minimal to no money down

GETTING FROM POINTS A TO B

GETTING FROM POINTS A TO B

Public transportation is the most cost effective way to get around. You avoid the car note, car insurance, gas and maintenance costs associated with car ownership. If you already own a car, using public transportation can lower your overall cost by reducing the cost of gas and expanding the time between maintenance due to lower mileage.

Check out the cost of a monthly, unlimited ride card for public transportation in the following large cities (just think of the gas and parking fee savings):

- Houston – METRO Card - $35
- Los Angeles – Metro Pass - $52
- Atlanta - MARTA Card- $52.50
- Chicago – CTA 30-Day Pass - $75
- New York – Metro Card - $ 76

If you are a student, you may ride free or receive up to 60 percent discounts on monthly public transportation passes. Check with your Office of Student Services or ask your fellow students.

If public transportation is not an option in your area, here are a few options to decrease your monthly transportation costs:

Option 1: Live really close to your job and walk or ride a bike

Option 2: Commute with a co-worker or a friend who works in the area. Decide on your contribution for gas and oil changes.

Option 3: Take advantage of the *Park and Ride* programs offered through your local transit authority.

Option 4: Save money to purchase a small previously owned car. Target no more than 75,000 miles. Consider the cost of repairs and maintenance when shopping for a car. If you don't know a lot about cars, bring a person with you who is familiar. Again, do your research!

Remember, access to transportation helps to determine where you choose to live, so explore all your options.

PUTTING FOOD ON THE TABLE

PUTTING FOOD ON THE TABLE

Unfortunately, many people go to bed hungry every night. The reason…they don't know the options available to them.

Fortunately, the USDA's Food and Nutrition Services offers a subsidies program. For now, it is called the Food Stamp Program but they are exploring a name change to, I believe, remove some of the stigma associated with the program.

In 2004, the program provided an average $86 per person or about $200 per family. Contrary to popular myth, you can have a job, although the total household income is limited. What's more, you can own a car with a fair market value up to $4650. However, there are exceptions if the vehicle is:

- Used over 50 percent of the time for income-producing purposes
- Needed for long distance travel to work
- Used as the home

If applying for government assistance frightens you, quite a few organizations offer discount food. One such program is Angel Food Ministries, a non-profit, non-denominational organization serving 32 states.

The organization sells a box (you provide the box) full of food on a monthly basis for $25. Check out what $25 bought in June 2005:

(1) 3 lb. Pork Spare Ribs	(1) 1 lb. Chicken Tenders
(4) 5 oz. Beef Short Ribs	(1) 17.5 oz. BBQ Sauce
(1) 4 lb. I.Q.F. Chicken Thighs	(1) 16 oz. Baked Beans
(1) 2 lb. Corn Dogs	(1) 7.5 oz. Mac & Cheese
(1) 1 lb. Meat Balls	(1) 18 oz. Sara Lee Bagels

(1) 8 oz. Cream Cheese   (1) 1 lb. Carrots
(1) 16 oz. Apple Sauce   (1) 16 oz. Green Peas
(1) 16 oz. Corn-on-the-Cob   (1) Dessert
(1) 3 lb. Potatoes   (1) Dozen Eggs

WOW!

Other options are available if both applying for government assistance AND ordering food through charitable organizations does not appeal to you.

Topping the list of options is clipping coupons and shopping at stores offering to double or triple your coupon value in addition to sales prices.

Right up there with coupons is buying meats in bulk then dividing into storage bags to freeze for later meals. Using this method can allow you to provide more meals for your money in the end.

For example:

	Retail Price/lb	Bulk Price/lb	Savings
10 lbs Ground Beef	$3.06	$0.99	$20.70
10 lbs Pork Chops	$3.20	$1.37	$18.30
10 lbs Chicken legs	$1.29	$0.79	$5

Source: U.S. Department of Labor: Bureau of Labor Statistics. Online at www.bls.gov.

With a purchase of 10 pounds of each meat staple monthly, you can save *$528 per year* or more by buying in bulk.

Eating smarter, you may want a vegetable with that meat. The high cost of fresh vegetables in grocery stores usually sends people to the can goods aisle with vegetables packed in sodium.

To purchase fresh vegetables at reasonable prices visit your local fruit stands. Often they are located near bus stops to attract low-income earners.

Another option is to start a vegetable garden. If you don't have enough yard for a garden, you can start a container vegetable garden. Using barrels, flowerpots, window boxes or baskets lined with ventilated plastic, you can grow carrots, radishes, lettuce, tomatoes and peppers among others. The seeds are not extremely expensive and you get a great supply of natural nutrients.

Now that you have food to cook, you need to decide how to prepare and distribute your food supplies.

One of the best ways is to cook one meal for the entire week. You know what you are having on a daily basis so there is less anxiety. Also, put a little up for your daily lunch. Taking a moment to do this can save you an average $5 per workday or $1300 or more per year.

Home cooking can be fun and healthy. Be creative with your meal preparation.

PAYING FOR DOCTOR VISITS

PAYING FOR DOCTOR VISITS

For low-income earning adults, going to a doctor occurs only when their symptoms are too bad to ignore. Mot believer going to a dentist is a luxury. But, there are options.

Federally funded, state-run healthcare is available through Medicaid, which gives qualified persons more options due to the number of private doctors that accept the card.

Medicaid pays for health care costs, including doctor's visits, dentist and eye care services. It includes mental health care and prescription drug coverage.

Qualifications vary from state to state but generally, you can qualify if one or more of the following is true:

- You have children and a limited income
- You receive or are eligible for Supplemental Security Income (SSI)
- You are a pregnant woman and meet income requirements
- Your family's assets are less than $2000
- You receive adoption assistance or foster care assistance
- You are under 18 (some states the age is under 21)

Children under 18 typically are covered by the State Children's Health Insurance Program (SCHIP), but as an adult, if you do not qualify for Medicaid and cannot afford private health insurance, Free Clinics and state funded hospitals provide free or low cost services based on your income.

Free Clinics are private, non-profit, community based organizations that provide medical, dental, prescription drug and/or mental health services. Volunteer health professionals and community members along with other health providers, partner to provide these services.

For vision services, VISION USA is a program in which volunteer doctors provide comprehensive eye exams at no charge and provide eyewear at little or no cost. Requirements for this service vary from state to state but you must:

- Have a job or live in a household where there is one working member;
- Have no vision insurance (this may include Medicare/Medicaid);
- Have income below an established level based on household size; and
- Not have had an eye exam within 2 years.

After you apply for services through VISION USA, it takes a few weeks to receive an appointment.

As you have seen, there are options for all your health care needs. Don't let a preventable or treatable illness persist because you don't believe you can get the assistance you need.

COVERING YOUR BODY AND FEET

COVERING YOUR BODY & FEET

The most obvious source of clothing is hand me downs from other relatives. However, if that is not a choice for you, previously used clothes ore the new word "resale" clothing is a good choice. The Salvation Army, Goodwill and other thrift stores and consignment shops sell clothing and other items at low cost. Previously worn designer clothes and shoes are sold at a small fraction of their retail price.

A list of stores is found in your local phone book or by contacting the National Association for Resale & Thrift Shops.

If the idea of previously worn clothing does not appeal to you, although most shops sell cleaned clothing, there are options that will not leave you completely broke.

Major department stores such as Macy's, offers extremely deep discounts on out-of-season clothing. If you shop ahead of time, you can find items such as $100 cashmere sweaters marked down to $20, designer jeans discounted by 75 percent and shoes as low as $5. Not to mention, discounts on suits and dresses can rise up to 80 percent during the off-season.

New shoes can be purchased at low prices from major discount stores, including Wal-Mart and Target in addition to regular department stores. Stores such as DFW, sells designer shoes for men and women at up to 75% off already reduced prices, year round. You can purchase $300 Prada shoes for as little as $75. Keep in mind, at minimum wage $75 is still a lot of money but if you save in other areas you may just chose to put that money to your clothing fund.

Shopping during the week can also save you tons on new clothes. On weekdays (Monday – Thursday), some stores offer deep discounts and "2 for 1" sales to attract customers to the stores. They may also have free giveaways on those days including popcorn and drinks. Check your local newspaper.

Keep your eyes open for sales and bargains. Sometimes a new item from a department store may cost less than the same item at a resale shop. Do your homework. Have fun shopping!

.

SEARCHING FOR ENTERTAINMENT

SEARCHING FOR ENTERTAINMENT

Old television shows and movies can provide a temporary distraction but sometimes you want to meet new people and develop friendships. Here are several categories of free or low cost entertainment options:

Category 1: Movies

Option 1: **Free movie screenings**. Local radio stations and organizations offer screenings to upcoming movies. Check your local alternative newspapers such as, Creative Loafing or the entertainment or living sections of your local newspaper for listings. Typically, these screenings are offered Monday through Wednesday.

Option 2: **Dollar theaters**. Just before going to video, quite few movies trickle through these low cost theaters. In some cities, these theaters show new movies at cost less than $5.

Option 3: **College theaters**. A number of colleges have movie theaters on campus that run new independent films. At times, they screen upcoming films or late-running blockbuster films. Visit the college's student center for information on policy regarding admission to non-students.

Category 2: Concerts/Festivals

Option 1: **Local radio/television stations**. These organizations offer free concerts to their listeners. For example, those in the New York City area can enjoy weekly concert series featuring popular music artists as local news programs compete for viewers. Visit the Web sites of your local stations or call their information line for schedules of concerts. *NOTE:* Some cities offer free concerts series featuring local and national artists. In the city of Atlanta, for instance, the city sponsors free noon and evening weekday concerts for a few months a year.

Option 2: **City festivals**. Countless cities have free admission festivals. Luckily, the local phone book lists these festivals in monthly order toward the front of the book. Your local newspaper can also be a valuable source of information. Festivals can range from arts and crafts to music festivals to carnivals.

Category 3: Parties

Option 1: **Dinner parties**. Potluck is the only way to go for dinner parties. Invite a few people over to bring a favorite food dish and enjoy good conversation.

Option 2: **Dessert parties**. Invite guests to bring a dessert. For an added twist, ask each person to bring an ingredient for a dessert that everyone can join in making. It makes for a great time for all.

Option 3: **Movie night**. Ask everyone to contribute $2 to pay for movie rental, popcorn and drinks. It is cheaper and more fun to use old-fashioned popping corn instead of microwave popcorn.

Option 4: **Game night**. Invite a few friends to bring a snack and/or a game. You can combine Game night with a Dessert party. Here are suggestions for games: board games, card games, charades, dominoes, checkers and chest. Playing these games as tournaments, with prizes from a local dollar gift shop, can add greater enjoyment.

Category 4: The Arts

Option 1: **Museums.** There are museums for any interest you may have including: history, culture, automobiles and science.

Option 2: **Art galleries.** Free galleries are located in most cities. On occasion, these galleries have showcase events that offer a cultural experience and free food and drinks. Your local newspaper is the best source for events.

Category 5: The Internet

Public libraries and public universities offer limited access for the public to use their Internet services free of charge. Watching movie trailers and music videos or reading newspapers and magazines are just a few uses of the Internet. Taking time to job hunt on the Internet is a great use of time for those with a desire to improve their financial situation. *NOTE*: Please check the rules of your local library.

These are not the only free or minimal cost entertainment options. Ask people around you what they do for fun. Many free activities are free because they depend on word of mouth advertising.

BEGINNING TO LIVE

Now that you have completed reading this guide you can go LIVE better and save more. Become an example to your family and friends who are feeling hopeless due to their pay rate.

REMEMBER: Your current pay rate does not determine your fate.

 You can change or transform your life.

RESOURCES

RESOURCES

HOUSING – check your telephone blue pages for local contact information
1. U.S. Department of Housing and Urban Development (HUD) www.hud.gov or www.espanol.hud.gov

2. Public Housing Authority- The Public Housing Authorities Directors Association (PHADA) is an advocate group that represents the professional administrators of housing authorities. The organization's Web site connects visitors to many local Public Housing Authority Web sites across the U.S. http://www.phada.org/linkha.html

TRANSPORTATION - check your telephone blue pages for local contact information
- Metropolitan Transit Authority of Harris County, Tx: (713) 635-4000 www.ridemetro.org
- Los Angeles Metropolitan Transit Authority: 1-800-COMMUTE www.mta.net
- Metropolitan Atlanta Rapid Transit Authority (MARTA): (404) 848-4711 www.itsmarta.com
- Chicago Transit Authority (CTA) 1-800-YOURCTA: www.transitchicago.com
- Metropolitan Transportation Authority – NY Transit (MTA): www.mta.nyc.ny.us/nyct/

FOOD
1. Check out the record of charities with the BBB Wise Giving Alliance program: (703) 276-0100 www.give.org

2. USDA's Food and Nutrition Services: www.fns.usda.gov/
   - Food Stamp Program - 1-800-221-5689

3. Angel Food Ministries – 1-888-819-3745 www.angelfoodministries.com

MEDICAL
1. State Children's Health Insurance Program (SCHIP): 1-877-267-2323 www.cms.hhs.gov/schip/

2. Insure Kids Now!: 1-800-Kids-Now www.insurekidsnow.gov/

3. Medicaid: 1-877-267-2323 www.cms.hhs.gov/medicaid/

Listing of state offices: Source: Centers for Medicare & Medicaid Services Web site
www.cms.hhs.gov/medicaid/allStateContacts.asp

State	Office Name	Address	Contact Phone
Alaska	Alaska Dept of Health and Social Services	350 Main Street, Room 229 P.O. Box 110601 Juneau, AK 99811-0601	Local: 1-907-465-3030
Alabama	Medicaid Agency of Alabama	501 Dexter Avenue P.O. Box 5624 Montgomery, AL 36103-5624	Local: 1-334-242-5000 Toll-Free: 1-800-362-1504
Arkansas	Dept of Human Services of Arkansas	P.O. Box 1437, Slot 1100 Donaghey Plaza South Little Rock, AR 72203-1437	Local: 1-501-682-8292 Toll-Free: 1-800-482-5431 (Eligibility call 1-800-482-8988) Spanish Phone: 1-800-482-8988 Local TTY: 1-501-682-6789
American Samoa	Dept of Human Services of Hawaii	P.O. Box 339 Honolulu, AS 96809	Local: 1-808-587-3521 (011-684-633-4590 or 011-684-633-4036 for AS) Local TTY: 1-808-692-7182
Arizona	Health Care Cost Containment of Arizona	801 E. Jefferson Phoenix, AZ 85034	Local: 1-602-417-4000 (Out of state: 1-800-523-0231) Toll-Free: 1-800-962-6690 Spanish Phone: 1-602-417-7700 Local TTY: 1-602-417-4191
California	California Dept of Health Services	P.O. Box 942732 Sacramento, CA 94234-7320	Local: 1-916-440-7400 Local TTY: 1-916-445-0553
Colorado	Dept of Health Care Policy and Financing of Colorado	1570 Grant Street Denver, CO 80203-1818	Local: 1-303-866-2993 Toll-Free: 1-800-221-3943 Spanish Phone: 1-303-866-1416 Local TTY: 1-303-866-3883
Connecticut	Dept of Social Services of Connecticut	25 Sigourney Street Hartford, CT 06106-5033	Local: 1-860-424-4908 Toll-Free: In-State Calls Only 1-800-842-1508
District of Columbia	DC Dept of Health	825 North Capitol Street, NE 5th Floor Washington, DC 20002	1-202-442-5999

State	Office Name	Address	Contact Phone
Delaware	Delaware Health and Social Services	1901 N. DuPont Highway P.O. Box 906, Lewis Bldg. New Castle, DE 19720	Local: 1-302-255-9040
Florida	Agency for Health Care Administration of Florida	P.O. Box 13000 Tallahassee, FL 32317-3000	Toll-Free: 1-888-419-3456
Georgia	Georgia Dept of Community Health	2 Peachtree Street, NW Atlanta, GA 30303	Local: 1-770-570-3300 Toll-Free: 1-866-322-4260
Hawaii	Dept of Human Services of Hawaii	P.O. Box 339 Honolulu, HI 96809	Local: 1-808-587-3521 (011-684-633-4590 or 011-684-633-4036 for AS) Local TTY: 1-808-692-7182
Iowa	Dept of Human Services of Iowa	Hoover State Office Building 5th Floor Des Moines, IA 50319-0114	Local: 1-515-327-5121 Toll-Free: 1-800-338-8366
Idaho	Idaho Dept of Health and Welfare	450 West State Street Boise, ID 83720-0036	Local: 1-208-334-5500 Toll-Free: 1-800-685-3757 Local TTY: 1-208-332-7205
Illinois	Dept of Public Aid of Illinois	201 South Grand Avenue, East Springfield, IL 62763	Local: 1-217-782-1200 Toll-Free: 1-800-226-0768 Spanish Phone: 1-217-785-8036 Local TTY: 1-800-526-5812
Indiana	Family and Social Services Administration of Indiana	402 W. Washington Street P.O. Box 7083 Indianapolis, IN 46207-7083	Local: 1-317-233-4455 Toll-Free: 1-800-889-9949 Spanish Phone: 1-317-234-0225
Kansas	Dept of Social and Rehabilitation Services of Kansas	915 SW Harrison Street Topeka, KS 66612	Local: 1-785-274-4200 Toll-Free: 1-800-766-9012 Local TTY: 1-785-296-1491
Kentucky	Cabinet for Health Services of Kentucky	P.O. Box 2110 Frankfort, KY 40602-2110	Local: 1-502-564-4321 Toll-Free: 1-800-635-2570
Louisiana	Louisiana Dept of Health and Hospital	1201 Capitol Access Road P.O. Box 629 Baton Rouge, LA 70821-0629	Local: 1-225-342-9500

State	Office Name	Address	Contact Phone
Massachusetts	Office of Health and Human Services of Massachusetts	600 Washington Street Boston, MA 02111	Local: 1-617-628-4141 (for provider only) Toll-Free: 1-800-841-2900
Maryland	Dept of Human Resources of Maryland	P.O. Box 17259 Baltimore, MD 21203-7259	Local: 1-410-767-5800 Toll-Free: 1-800-492-5231
Maine	Maine Dept of Health and Human Services	442 Civic Center Drive 11 State House Station Augusta, ME 04333-0011	Local: 1-207-624-7539 (Eligibility) Toll-Free: 1-800-977-6740 (option 2) Local TTY: 1-207-287-1828
Michigan	Michigan Dept Community Health	Sixth Floor, Lewis Cass Building 320 South Walnut Street Lansing, MI 48913	Local: 1-517-373-3740 Local TTY: 1-517-373-3573
Minnesota	Dept of Human Services of Minnesota	444 Lafayette Road North St. Paul, MN 55155	Local: 1-651-297-3933 Toll-Free: 1-800-333-2433 Local TTY: 1-651-296-5705
Missouri	Dept of Social Services of Missouri	221 West High Street P.O. Box 1527 Jefferson City, MO 65102-1527	Local: 1-573-751-4815 Toll-Free: In-State Calls Only 1-800-392-2161
Mississippi	Office of the Governor of Mississippi	239 North Lamar Street, Suite 801 Robert E. Lee Bldg. Jackson, MS 39201-1399	Local: 1-601-359-6050 Toll-Free: 1-800-421-2408
Montana	Montana Dept of Public Health & Human Services-Division of Child and Adult Health Resources	1400 Broadway, Cogswell Building P.O. Box 8005 Helena, MT 59604-8005	Local: 1-406-444-4540 Toll-Free: In-State Calls Only 1-800-362-8312
North Carolina	North Carolina Dept of Health and Human Services	Division of Medical Assistance 2501 Mail Service Center Raleigh, NC 27699-2501	Local: 1-919-855-4100 Toll-Free: 1-800-662-7030 Local TTY: 1-877-733-4851
North Dakota	Dept of Human Services of North Dakota - Medical Services	600 E. Boulevard Avenue Bismarck, ND 58505-0250	Local: 1-701-328-2321 Toll-Free: In-State Calls Only 1-800-755-2604 Local TTY: 1-701-328-8950
Nebraska	Nebraska Dept of Health and Human Services System	P.O. Box 95044 Lincoln, NE 68509-5044	Local: 1-402-471-3121 Toll-Free: 1-800-430-3244 Local TTY: 1-402-471-9570

State	Office Name	Address	Contact Phone
New Hampshire	New Hampshire Dept of Health and Human Services	129 Pleasant Street Concord, NH 03301-3857	Local: 1-603-271-4238
New Jersey	Dept of Human Services of New Jersey	Quakerbridge Plaza, Building 6 P.O. Box 716 Trenton, NJ 08625-0716	Local: 1-609-588-2600 Toll-Free: In-State Calls Only 1-800-356-1561 Spanish Phone: In-State Calls Only 1-609-588-3844
New Mexico	Dept of Human Services of New Mexico	P.O. Box 2348 Sante Fe, NM 87504-2348	Local: 1-505-827-3100 Toll-Free: 1-888-997-2583 Spanish Phone: 1-800-432-6217 Local TTY: 1-505-827-3184
Nevada	Nevada Dept of Human Resources, Aging Division	1100 East William Street Suite 101 Carson City, NV 89701	Local: 1-775-684-7200
New York	New York State Dept of Health	Office of Medicaid Management Governor Nelson A. Rockefeller Empire State Plaza, Corning Tower Building Albany, NY 12237	Local: 1-518-747-8887 Toll-Free: 1-800-541-2831
Ohio	Dept of Job and Family Services of Ohio - Ohio Health Plans	30 East Broad Street 31st Floor Columbus, OH 43215-3414	Local: 1-614-728-3288 Toll-Free: 1-800-324-8680
Oklahoma	Health Care Authority of Oklahoma	4545 N. Lincoln Boulevard Suite 124 Oklahoma City, OK 73105	Local: 1-405-522-7171 (also (405) 522-7300) Toll-Free: 1-800-522-0310 Local TTY: 1-405-522-7179
Oregon	Oregon Dept of Human Services	500 Summer Street, NE 3rd Floor Salem, OR 94310-1014	Local: 1-503-945-5772 Toll-Free: 1-800-527-5772 Local TTY: 1-503-945-5895
Pennsylvania	Dept of Public Welfare of Pennsylvania	Health and Welfare Building, Rm 515 P.O. Box 2675 Harrisburg, PA 17105	Local: 1-717-787-1870 Toll-Free: 1-800-692-7462 Local TTY: 1-717-705-7103
Puerto Rico	Medicaid Office of Puerto Rico and Virgin Islands	GPO Box 70184 San Juan, PR 00936	Local: 1-787-250-0453
Rhode Island	Dept of Human Services of Rhode Island	Louis Pasteur Building 600 New London Avenue Cranston, RI 02921	Local: 1-401-462-5300 Spanish Phone: 1-401-462-1500 Local TTY: 1-401-462-3363

State	Office Name	Address	Contact Phone
South Carolina	South Carolina Dept of Health and Human Services	P.O. Box 8206 Columbia, SC 29202-8206	Local: 1-803-898-2500
South Dakota	Dept of Social Services of South Dakota	700 Governors Drive Richard F Kneip Bldg, Pierre, SD 57501	Local: 1-605-773-3495 Toll-Free: 1-800-452-7691 (Providers Only) Spanish Phone: 1-800-305-9673
Tennessee	Dept of Finance and Administration of Tennessee	729 Church Street Nashville, TN 37247	Local: 1-615-741-0192 Toll-Free: 1-800-669-1851 Local TTY: 1-615-313-9240
Texas	Health and Human Services Commission of Texas	4900 N. Lamar Boulevard 4th Floor Austin, TX 78701	Local: 1-512-424-6500 Toll-Free: 1-888-834-7406 Local TTY: 1-512-407-3250
Utah	Utah Dept of Health	288 North 1460 West P.O. Box 143101 Salt Lake City, UT 84114-3101	Local: 1-801-538-6155 Toll-Free: 1-800-662-9651 Spanish Phone: 1-800-662-9651
Virginia	Dept of Medical Assistance Services	600 East Broad Street Suite 1300 Richmond, VA 23219	Local: 1-804-786-6273 Toll-Free: In-State Calls Only 1-800-552-8627
US Virgin Islands	Medicaid Office of Puerto Rico and Virgin Islands	GPO Box 70184 San Juan, VI 00936	Local: 1-787-250-0453
Vermont	Agency of Human Services of Vermont	103 South Main Street Waterbury, VT 05676-1201	Local: 1-802-241-2800 Toll-Free: In-State Calls Only 1-800-250-8427 Local TTY: 1-802-241-1282
Washington	Dept of Social and Health Services of Washington	P.O. Box 45505 Olympia, WA 98504-5505	Local: 1-800-562-6188 Toll-Free: In-State Calls Only 1-800-562-3022
Wisconsin	Wisconsin Dept of Health and Family Services	1 West Wilson Street P.O. Box 309 Madison, WI 53701-0309	Local: 1-608-221-5720 Toll-Free: 1-800-362-3002 Local TTY: 1-608-267-7371
West Virginia	West Virginia Dept of Health & Human Resources	350 Capitol Street Room 251 Charleston, WV 25301-3709	Local: 1-304-558-1700
Wyoming	Wyoming Dept of Health	147 Hathaway Building Cheyenne, WY 82002	Local: 1-307-777-7531 Local TTY: 1-307-777-5578

4. National Association of Free Clinics: www.nafclinics.org/ or www.freeclinics.us

5. American Optometric Association VISION USA: 1-800-766-4466 www.aoa.org/x1061.xml

CLOTHING/SHOES – see your local yellow pages for telephone numbers

1. National Association for Resale & Thrift Shops: http://www.narts.org/

2. Salvation Army: www.satruck.com

3. Goodwill: http://locator.goodwill.org/

COMING SOON:

SUPPLEMENTAL BOOKLETS

Order Now!

Entertainment Options. (*Customized for your area.*) $10 [EO]

101 Cheap Recipes $10 [CR]

35 Activities for Families $5 [FA]

or

Order additional copies of *How to LIVE on Minimum Wage* for $13.95
  (For discounts on bulk orders of 26 or more, email bulk@mazuliopub.com)

To order, please send a check or money order made payable to the
author, Tiffany Green.
                              Mail to:
                           Tiffany Green
                               LOF
                           P.O. Box 1831
                         Atlanta, GA 30301

Name _____
Mailing Address _____
Phone number _____ email: _____
Requested City _____Largest city nearby _____
#Brochures ___EO ___CR ___FA
#Copies of books ___   Total amount included _____
                              (Allow 2-4 weeks for delivery)

www.ingramcontent.com/pod-product-compliance
Lightning Source LLC
Chambersburg PA
CBHW021928170526
45157CB00005B/2237